# THE ULTIMATE BEGINNER S

# BASS BASICS

## Revised Edition

**Dale Titus • Albert Nigro**

**Alfred** Music Publishing Co., Inc.
P.O. Box 10003
Van Nuys, CA 91410-0003
**alfred.com**

ISBN-10: 0-7390-8197-7 (Book & CD)
ISBN-13: 978-0-7390-8197-6 (Book & CD)

ISBN-10: 0-7390-8204-3 (Book, CD & DVD)
ISBN-13: 978-0-7390-8204-1 (Book, CD & DVD)

ISBN-10: 0-7579-8166-6 (DVD)
ISBN-13: 978-0-7579-8166-1 (DVD)

Cover photographs:
Bass courtesy of Fender Musical Instruments Corporation.
Blue energy © iStockphoto.com / Raycat

# Contents

# Introduction

The bass: it's such a fun and versatile instrument to play. As a member of the rhythm section, the bass helps to drive the band and define the harmony for the song, but it can also step into the spotlight and take a solo or even play a melody. This book covers the fundamentals you'll need to start on your journey towards mastering this instrument: the various parts of the bass, how to tune and restring, how to develop good picking and fretting techniques, great exercises that will develop strength and dexterity in both hands, and how to create and play some common bass lines. This book also provides some helpful tips on how to practice, and all of the exercises have been recorded for you to hear and play along with.

**Introduction**
Track 1

**Tuning Notes**
Track 2

Photo by Joe Sia/Courtesy of Star File Photo, Inc.

*Victor Wooten is one of the foremost virtuoso bassists of his generation. Born into a musical family, he was playing gigs by age five with the Wooten Brothers Band. In 1988, he joined Béla Fleck and the Flecktones, along with his brother Roy "Future Man" Wooten. Victor soon became well-known in the bass community and beyond for the ease with which he performed the intricate compositions of the Flecktones. Their unique music defies classification, drawing from jazz, bluegrass, funk, and beyond. Wooten is widely regarded as a technical innovator who revolutionized the slap & pop technique. He continues to collaborate with Béla Fleck and also performs as a solo artist and with his brothers.*

Photo by Edward Lines Jr./ courtesy of Star File Photo, Inc.

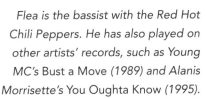

*Flea is the bassist with the Red Hot Chili Peppers. He has also played on other artists' records, such as Young MC's* Bust a Move *(1989) and Alanis Morrisette's* You Oughta Know *(1995).*

## Types of Basses

Track 3

### FOUR-STRING

This is a four-string fretted bass. The four-string is the most commonly played bass today. Because of its simple design and versatility, the four-string bass is a great instrument for beginners.

### FRETLESS BASS

This is a fretless bass. Because it has no frets on the fingerboard, the fretless has a very distinctive sound. Some fretless basses have fret positions marked on the neck, but they don't have frets (see photo). The fretless bass is also much harder to play, so it is not recommended for beginners. If you happen to have a fretless, the information in this book will still be useful to you.

## FIVE- AND SIX-STRING BASSES

The five- and six-string basses are relatively new to the public, but are quickly gaining popularity. The extra strings allow players to cover a wider range of pitches. Because of their wider necks and higher selling prices, most five- and six-string basses are not recommended for someone who's just starting out.

## STRINGS

Bass strings are available in three basic gauges: light (soft), medium, and heavy. Start with a light to medium gauge set of strings. An approximate starting gauge is .040 for the G string, .060 for the D string, .075–.080 for the A string, and .095–.100 for the E string.

# Parts of the Bass

Track 4

- Headstock
- Tuning pegs
- Nut
- Fingerboard
- Frets
- Position markers
- Neck
- 4th string
- 1st string
- Strap button
- Body
- Pickup
- Bridge
- Volume and tone controls
- Input jack

# Amplifiers

When you're first starting out, look for an amplifier that's reliable, has a good-sized speaker and has the most power that you can afford to buy. Power is not just for volume; it's also for clarity, and it is important to get as much as you can. If you have no idea where to start, go to your bass instructor or ask a trusted friend that plays bass. Then, go down to a music store and play everything they have, ask questions, and make an informed decision.

*Amp head and cabinet by Epiphone. Heads and cabinets can be mixed and matched to suit your tastes.*

*SWR combo amp. All of the components are built into the one piece.*

# How to Tune Up

## ELECTRIC TUNERS

Many brands of small battery-operated tuners, similar to the one shown below, are available. Simply follow the instructions supplied with your tuner.

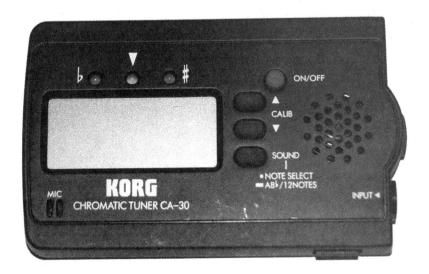

## TUNING TO A PIANO OR ELECTRONIC KEYBOARD

An easy way to tune a bass is to a piano keyboard. The four strings of the bass are tuned to the keyboard notes shown in the following diagram:

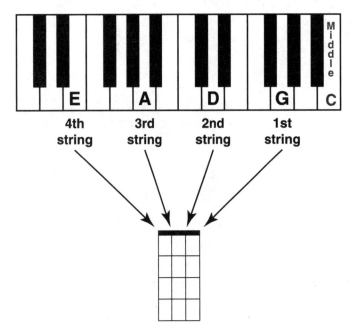

## TUNING THE BASS TO ITSELF (RELATIVE TUNING)

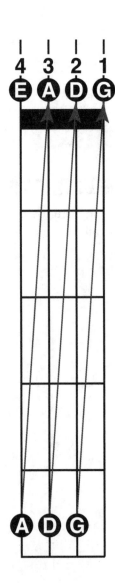

1.  Tune the 1st string to G on the piano (or some other fixed pitch instrument, such as a pitch pipe).

2.  Depress the 2nd string at the 5th fret. Play it and you will hear the note G, the same as the 1st string open. Turn the 2nd string tuning key until the pitch of the 2nd string matches that of the 1st string.

3.  Depress the 3rd string at the 5th fret. Play it and you will hear the note D, the same as the 2nd string open. Turn the 3rd string tuning key until the pitch of the 3rd string matches that of the 2nd string.

4.  Depress the 4th string at the 5th fret. Play it and you will hear the note A, the same as the 3rd string open. Turn the 4th string tuning key until the pitch of the 4th string matches that of the 3rd string.

# TUNING BY HARMONICS

Another method of tuning is the harmonic method, which is a little more accurate because the tone is very pure and higher in pitch, making it easier to hear when the notes are in tune than using open strings. To play a harmonic on the bass, lightly touch the string directly over a fret (do not depress the string to the fretboard). Pluck with the picking hand. You should hear a ringing "bell-like" sound.

## To TUNE USING HARMONICS

1.  Play the harmonic on the 5th fret of the E string. This should match the harmonic on the 7th fret of the A string.

2.  Once those strings are in tune, match the harmonic on the 5th fret of the A string to that on the 7th fret of the D string.

3.  Finally, repeat this using the harmonics on the 5th fret of the D string and the 7th fret of the G string.

Listen for the waves to slow down and eventually stop when the strings are in tune. This method can also be used with electronic tuners. If the tuner doesn't respond well to the open strings, try using the harmonics at the 12th fret of each string instead. The higher pitch and clearer tone usually provide a better signal from the instrument to the tuner.

# Changing Strings

There are a few reasons you may have to change your strings: One, of course, is if you break a string. Another is that strings will become dull sounding and harder to tune the longer you play them, so eventually they'll have to be replaced.

## To REPLACE A STRING

1.  Remove the old string. Do not remove all the old strings from your bass at once because this releases too much tension, which is bad for the neck. It is safer to remove only one string at a time. Also, it is better to loosen the strings with the tuning keys rather than cut them with wire cutters. Save the old strings as spares in case a new one breaks.

2.  After the old string has been removed, the new string is seated to the bridge; that is, the ball end is placed through the tailpiece and over the saddles of the bridge. On some models, the string must be pulled through the tailpiece. Be careful to put the correct string in the correct place as the different strings each have a different tension.

3.  Stretch the string along the fingerboard. Insert it into the proper tuning key and tighten either by hand or with a peg winder, keeping tension on the string and making sure each winding around the post is towards the headstock, not the tip of the post.

On models with a split tuning key, a small amount of excess string should be cut off the tip to allow proper fit on the post, generally 2½ to 3 inches above the tuning key post. Insert the tip of the string into the hole and bend the string into the slot on the post.

The strings should wind to the outside of the post, and each string should be seated the correct slot in the nut. After changing the string there will be a period in which the string will stretch. This can be hastened by pulling on the string or simply by playing.

# Note Names on the Fingerboard

It's vital to know where all the notes are located on the bass. This will make jamming with other musicians much easier. It has been said that there is no real money above the 5th fret; although that is meant as a joke, it's true that a bass payer can do a lot of playing within the first five frets. Most of the exercises in this book stay within the first five frets.

## THE MUSICAL ALPHABET  Track 5

The musical alphabet is made up of seven natural notes named for the first seven letters of the alphabet (A–G). After G, we begin again with A. All notes are separated by a whole step, except for the notes E–F and B–C, which are separated by a *half step*. On the bass, a half step is equal to one fret, and a *whole step* is equal to two frets.

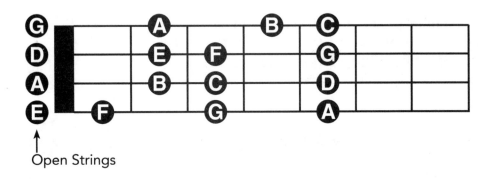

Open Strings

The notes in between the natural notes have names relating to them. For instance, the note between F and G is called either F *sharp* (indicated by the ♯ sign) or G *flat* (indicated by the ♭ sign), depending on the direction the notes are heading. Sharps raise the note a half step (up one fret) and flats lower the note a half step (down one fret).

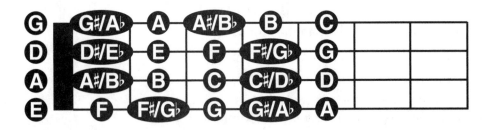

As shown in the tuning section, a note or pitch can be found in more than one location on the neck. Practice locating the same note on more than one string.

# Music Notation

## THE STAFF AND MEASURES

The rhythms and note names are indicated by standard music notation, and the location of those notes on the neck of the bass is indicated by tablature. Here are some basic rules of standard notation:

Music is written on a staff, which consists of five lines and four spaces (between the lines):

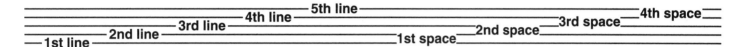

At the beginning of the staff is a bass clef (or F clef). The bass clef is used for all bass instruments.

The notes are written on the staff in alphabetical order. The first line is G:

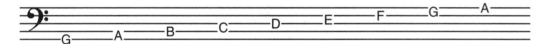

The staff is divided into *measures* by *bar lines*. A heavy *double bar line* marks the end of the music:

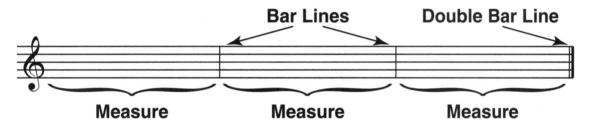

## TABLATURE (TAB)

Tablature is commonly used in conjunction with standard music notation. Tablature illustrates the location of notes on the neck of the bass. This illustration compares the four strings of a bass to the four lines of tablature.

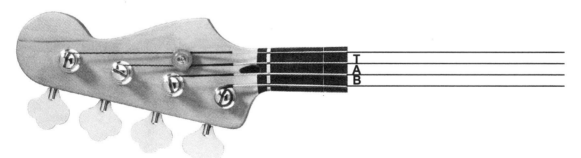

Notes are indicated by placing fret numbers on the strings. An "0" indicates an open string.

This tablature indicates to play the open, 1st, and 3rd frets on the 1st string.

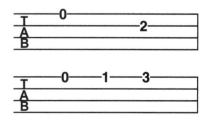

# Rhythm Notation and Time Signatures

At the beginning of every song is a time signature. $\frac{4}{4}$ is the most common time signature:

$\frac{4}{4}$   = FOUR COUNTS TO A MEASURE
= A QUARTER NOTE RECEIVES ONE COUNT

The top number tells you how many counts per measure.
The bottom number tells you which kind of note receives one count.

The time value of a note is determined by three things:

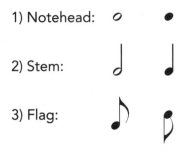

1) Notehead:

2) Stem:

3) Flag:

This is a whole note. The notehead is open and has no stem. In $\frac{4}{4}$ time, a whole note receives 4 counts.

This is a half note. It has an open notehead and a stem. A half note receives two counts.

This is a quarter note. It has a solid notehead and a stem. A quarter note receives one count.

This is an eighth note. It has a solid notehead and a stem with a flag attached. An eighth note receives one half count.

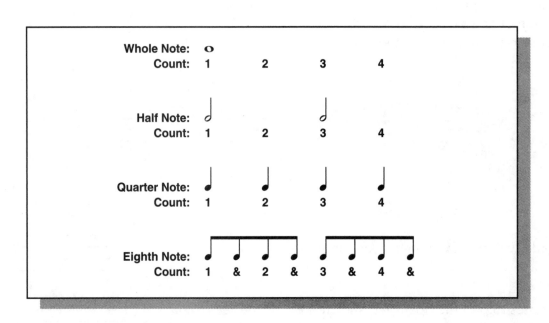

# Picking and Right-Hand Techniques

There are basically two ways to pluck the string: one is to use an actual pick, and the other is to play with two fingers of the right hand: the index and middle fingers. The pick gives a brighter sound with more attack and can be manipulated easier at faster tempos. The two-finger method is the most common, producing a warm and distinctive sound. When using this method, anchor your thumb to the bass, usually to the pickup. It is also important to alternate the right-hand attack, either by picking down and up with the pick (indicated ⊓ and ∨) or alternating the index and middle fingers (indicated *i* and *m*).

Track 6

 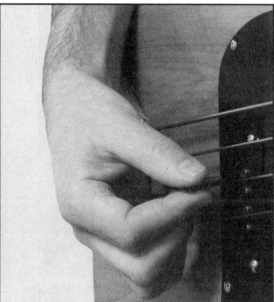

### EXAMPLE 1 – OPEN-STRING EXERCISE

Track 7

This exercise concentrates on the right hand exclusively. Mute the strings with your left hand by gently holding the strings without actually fretting them. Remember to alternate the picking in the right hand.

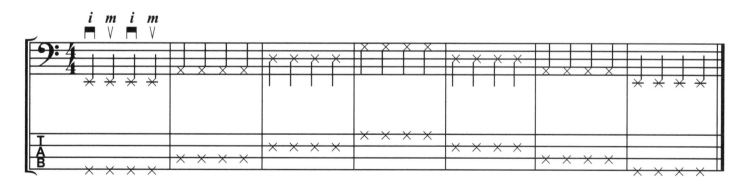

# Fretting Techniques

Once some coordination is established with the right hand, it is time to move on to the left hand to develop some basic fretting techniques. There are a few rules to keep in mind while practicing:

 Track 8

1. Keep the thumb on the back of the neck.

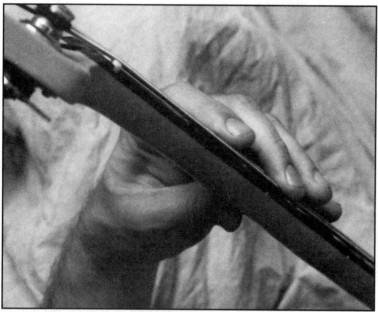

2. Leave a space between the palm of the left hand and the neck, not gripping too tightly.

3. Try to keep a one-finger-per-fret spacing with your left hand.

4. Play just behind, not directly on, the fret whenever possible.

**EXAMPLE 2 – FINGERBOARD EXERCISE**
Track 9

This simple exercise helps to develop good, clean fretting technique. While doing this exercise, make sure to alternate the right-hand fingers (or pick) consistently.

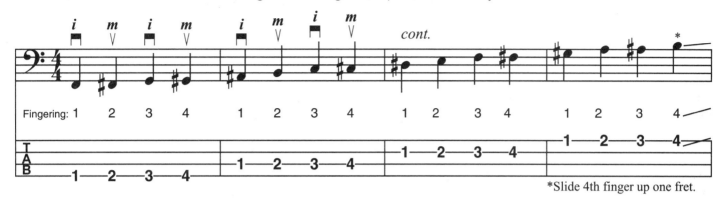

*Slide 4th finger up one fret.

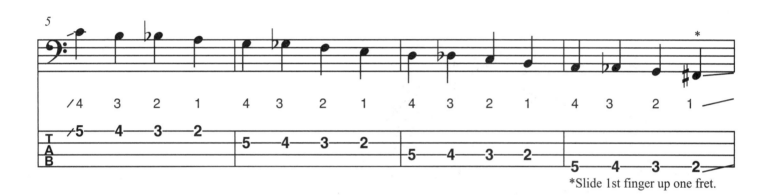

*Slide 1st finger up one fret.

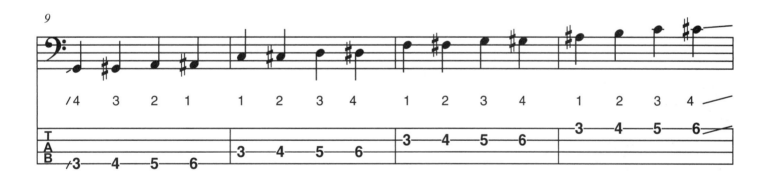

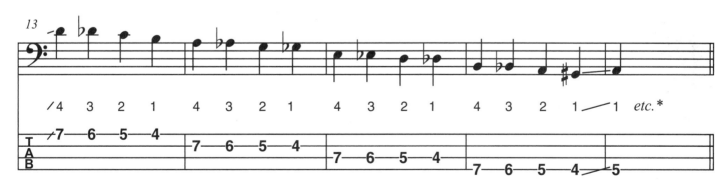

\* Continue pattern up
 the neck.

This is also a great exercise to develop technique up and down the neck of the bass. Spend about five minutes each day going through it to develop strong, consistent technique.

# Common Bass Lines

Let's talk about how to create some common bass lines. First of all, in many musical situations, the one note the bass player plays the most is the *root* of whatever chord is being played at the time. The root of a chord is the note on which the chord is built, and is where the chord gets its name (the root of a C chord is C).

 Track 10

Occasionally, bass players want to play some other notes to add color to their bass lines, so they turn to other chord tones besides the root, called *arpeggios*, to find which notes to use. An arpeggio is made up from the notes of a chord played one at a time. Let's start with the arpeggio of a very common chord type: the major chord.

## THE MAJOR CHORD  Track 11

The notes of a major arpeggio are the root, the third, and the fifth. The third of a C major chord is three notes up the C major scale (C–D–E) and the fifth is five notes up the C major scale (C–D–E–F–G).

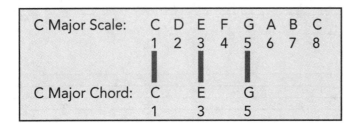

An easy way to play the major arpeggio is to play the root with the 2nd finger of the fretting hand. That makes the third easily reachable using the 1st finger, and the 4th finger can easily grab the fifth. This is great because you can move this arpeggio around just by knowing the root of the chord you're playing against. Practice this arpeggio pattern over C and then transpose it to G and D.

### C Major Arpeggio

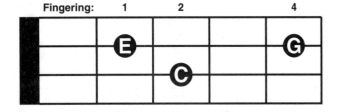

### G Major Arpeggio

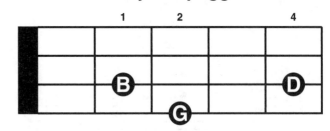

### D Major Arpeggio

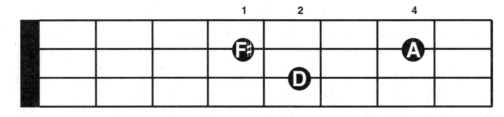

 **EXAMPLE 3 – G, C AND D MAJOR**
Track 12

This example demonstrates three ways to create a bass line using the major arpeggio with the roots G, C, and D. First, it gives just the root of each chord (Ex. 3A), then the straight arpeggio (Ex. 3B), next a little rhythmic variation that is similar to a common blues bass line (Ex. 3C), and finally a combination of these techniques (Ex. 3D). Play along with the rhythm track provided. Also, notice the sharp sign ♯ at the beginning of the music, right after the clef. This is called a *key signature*. It means the note on that line is played as a sharp (in this case, F♯), whenever it appears.

## EXAMPLE 3A – ROOT ONLY

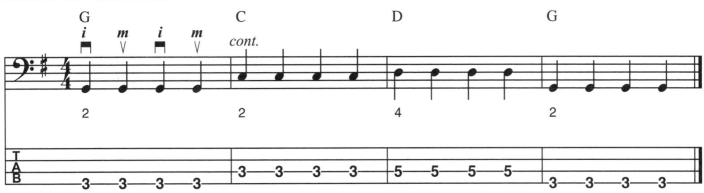

## EXAMPLE 3B – MAJOR ARPEGGIO

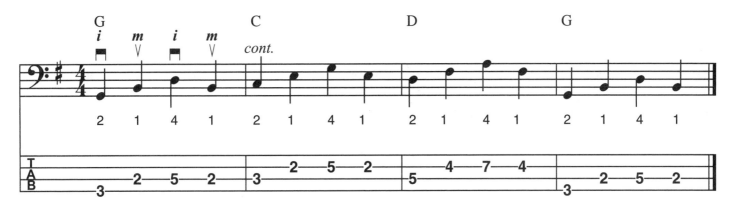

## EXAMPLE 3C – RHYTHMIC VARIATION

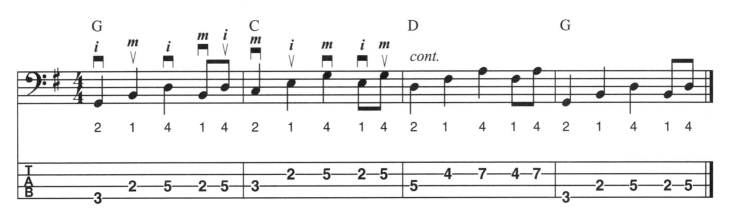

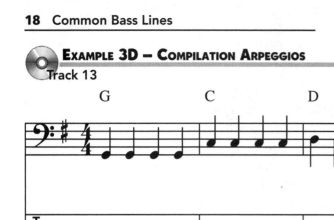

If while playing along you find it hard keeping up with the track, practice the patterns more slowly, until they become comfortable. It is important to always use a metronome or drum machine to maintain consistent time.

# THE MINOR CHORD Track 14

The minor chord is different than the major chord. The minor chord consists of the root, the flat third (a half step below the major chord third) and the fifth.

\* A *scale* is an arrangement of notes in a specific arrangement of half steps and whole steps.

The following fingering pattern is perfect for the minor chord arpeggio because you can always start it with your first finger pointing at the root.

### C Minor Arpeggio

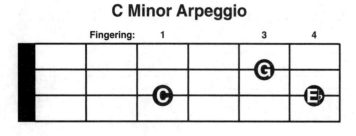

### G Minor Arpeggio

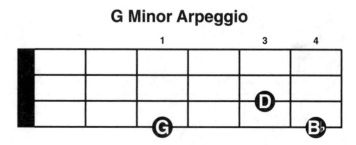

**Example 4 – Am–Dm–Bm–Em Arpeggios**

Track 15

This example demonstrates the minor arpeggio using the roots A, D, B and E. Like Example 3, Example 4 first gives the root only (Ex. 4A), then the minor arpeggio (Ex. 4B), next a slight variation of the arpeggio similar to a popular bass line (Ex. 4C), and finally a combination of these three techniques (Ex. 4D). This example also uses open string roots, so the fingering pattern is different from the "moveable fingering pattern." The patterns you already learned are called moveable because they can be played anywhere on the neck. Patterns with open strings are not moveable. The diagram below shows the minor arpeggio with the open 3rd string (A) as the root.

## A Minor Arpeggio

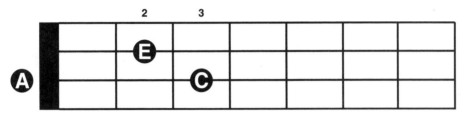

**Example 4A – Root Only**

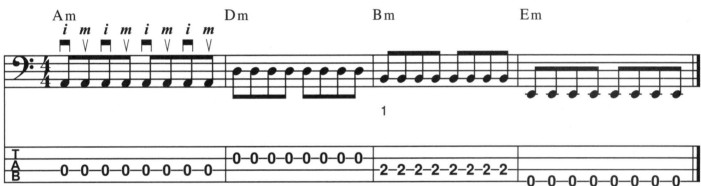

**Example 4B – Minor Arpeggio**

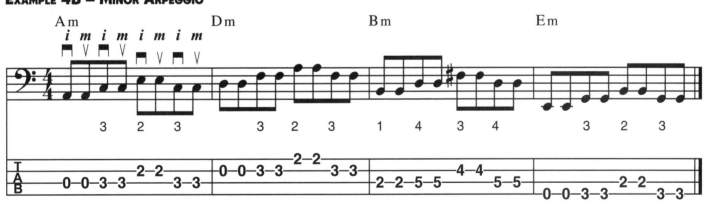

**Example 4C – Rhythmic Variation**

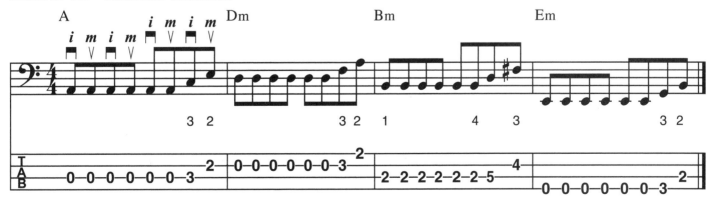

**EXAMPLE 4D – COMPILATION**
Track 16

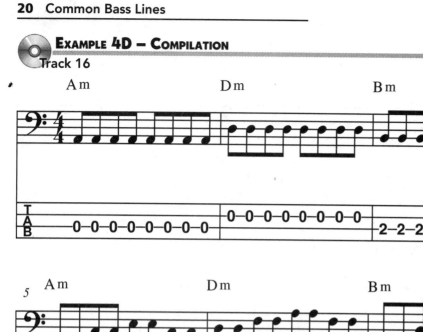

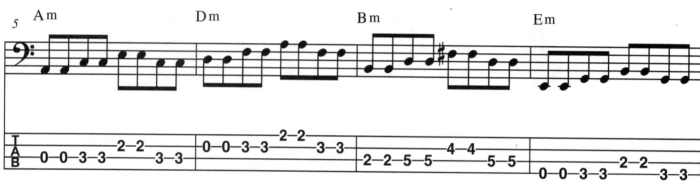

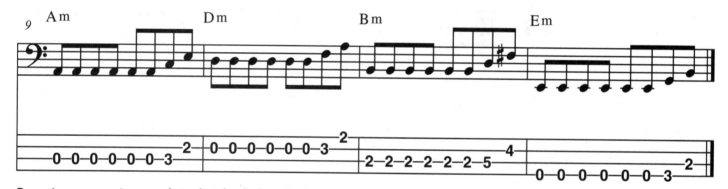

Practice repeating each individual chord separately to help develop technique and confidence.

## EXAMPLE 5

This example uses both major and minor chord arpeggios, and is based on a popular *chord progression*. A chord progression is a series of particular chords following a certain pattern. This particular progression can be found in songs such as "Blue Moon" and "Heart and Soul."

## EXAMPLE 5A

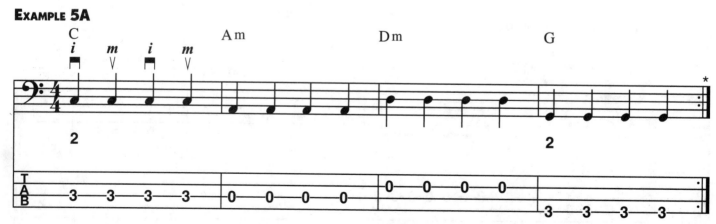

\* These two dots indicate a *repeat* sign, which means to go back to the beginning and play again.

**EXAMPLE 5B**

**EXAMPLE 5C**

**EXAMPLE 5D** Track 17

For further study on arpeggios, practice identifying the major and minor arpeggios all over the neck. Just be sure to use the same patterns and be able to identify the root.

# Playing with a Drummer

As members of a band, the bassist and drummer need to be a tight, indivisible team. The bass player needs to be sure that what he plays locks in with what the drummer is playing. One way to do this is to focus in on one particular part of the drum kit, such as the bass drum or snare, and play so that it and the bass sound as one instrument. Following are several common patterns to help you practice this.

Track 18

## Example 6 – Ballad Pattern
Track 19

This first pattern is a common ballad feel. Play the root of the C chord with the bass drum (Ex. 6A), then when that feels comfortable, play the fifth of the C chord (G) with the snare (Ex. 6B), and, finally, alternate between the two patterns (Ex. 6C).

### Example 6A

### Example 6B – Adding 5th (G) with Snare

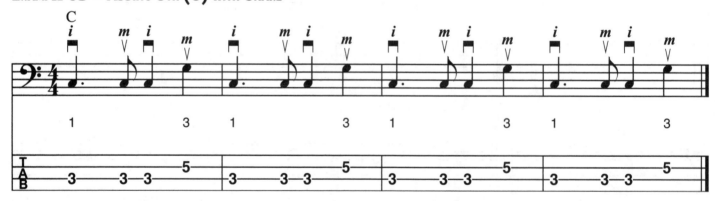

### Example 6C – Variation

Track 20

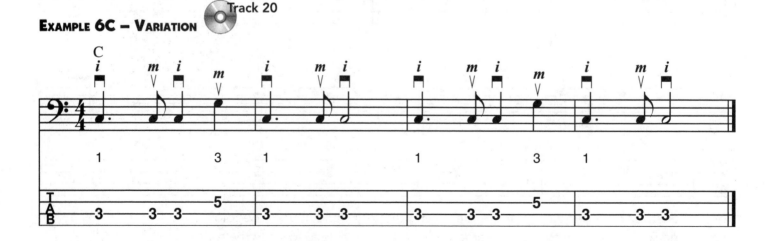

The previous example is a very common bass line to use when playing ballads: the root to the fifth above. However, the fifth can also be played below the root. The lower fifth is played on the same fret as the root, on the next lowest string. For example, the fifth of the C chord can be found on the third fret of the E string.

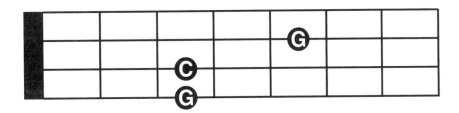

The fifths on the E string and D string are the same note, only an octave (8 notes) apart.

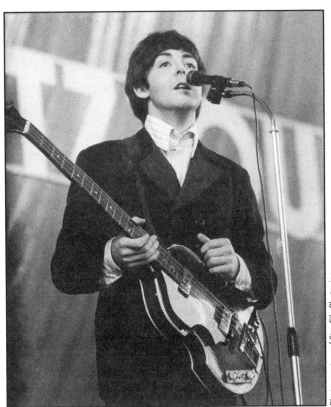

*Paul McCartney's use of melodic bass lines in songs with the Beatles was revolutionary for its time. His influence on bassists can still be heard in contemporary rock.*

**EXAMPLE 7 – COUNTRY PATTERN**
Track 21

One style that uses the fifth below the root is country. This exercise uses the root with
the bass drum (Ex. 7A), then adds the fifth below, this time also with the bass drum (Ex.
7B), and finally combines the two previous examples (Ex. 7C).

**EXAMPLE 7A – ROOT WITH BASS DRUM**

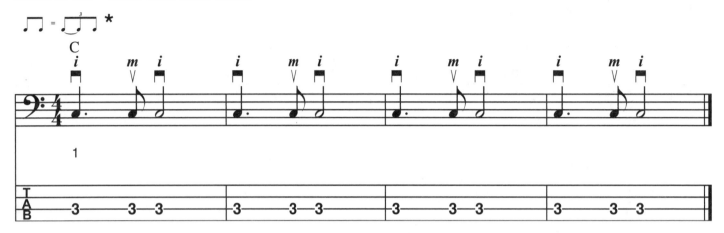

**\*** Indicates uneven eighth notes; listen to the recorded example.

**EXAMPLE 7B – ADDING 5TH BELOW**

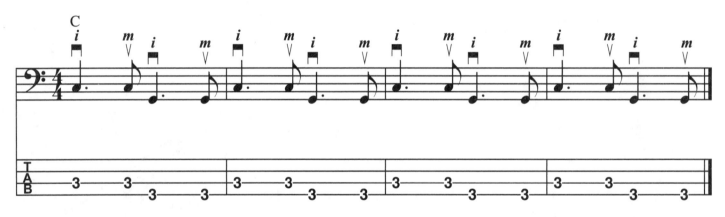

Track 22

**EXAMPLE 7C – COMBINATION**

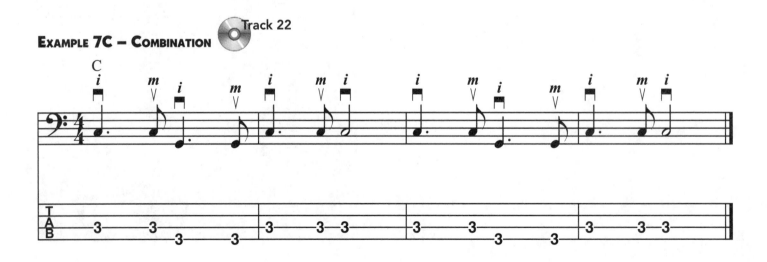

**Example 8 — Latin Pattern**

Track 23

This pattern uses both the fifth above and below, and is commonly used in Latin bass lines. The first part of the example gives just the root (Ex. 8A), then adds the fifth above (Ex. 8B), and finally the fifth both above and below (Ex. 8C).

**Example 8A — Root with Bass Drum/Latin**

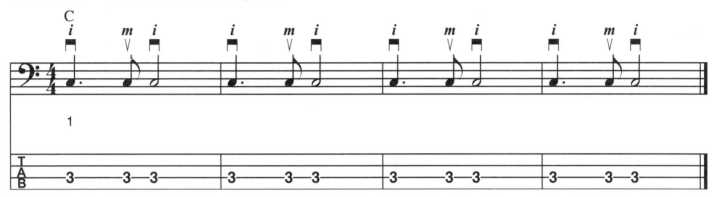

**Example 8B — Adding 5th Above**

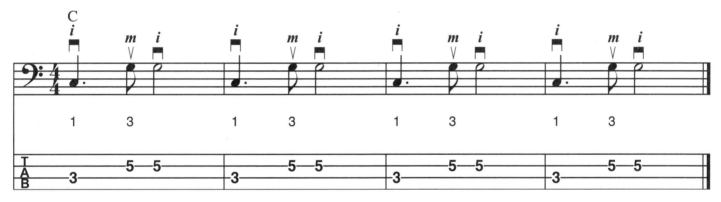

Track 24

**Example 8C — Adding 5th Above and Below**

Work on alternating the picking hand and developing a clean attack. Practicing these exercises should help you to lock in with the drummer, but always use a metronome or drum machine to maintain consistent time.

**EXAMPLE 9**

Track 25

This exercise uses the root to the fifth, both above and below. The chord progression is common to many popular songs and fits with many different rhythmic feels.

*1st ending: play the first time only and repeat*

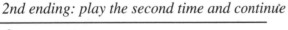

*2nd ending: play the second time and continue*

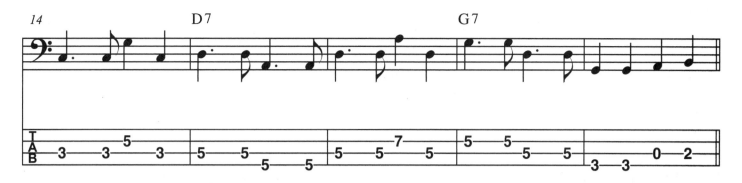

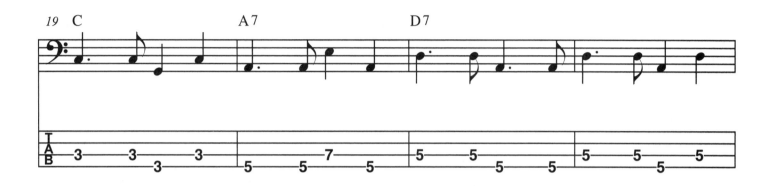

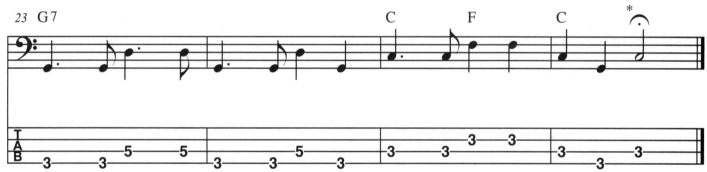

*The fermata indicates to hold the
note for an indefinite period of time.

Practice locating fifths above and below all notes on the neck, and familiarize yourself
with the patterns of both. Remember to keep alternating the right-hand fingering.

# Playin' the Blues

The blues is one of the most popular music styles. It's not very hard to play, but it is a lot of fun. It is a good idea to practice the blues, as most jam sessions usually contain at least one blues song. A blues bass line is easy to get under your fingers initially, so you can start jamming right away.

Track 26

## EXAMPLE 10
Track 27

This example uses the G major chord arpeggio: root, third and fifth, but adds the sixth and flat seventh on the D string, walking up the notes and back down again. The sixth of a G major chord is six notes up the G major scale (G–A–B–C–D–E), and the flat seventh is seven notes up the G major scale (G–A–B–C–D–E–F♯), lowered a half step to F♮. Note: When you "flat" the seventh, you lower it one half step. If F♯ is the seventh, then F is the flat seventh, not F♭.

| G Major Scale: | G | A | B | C | D | E | F♯ | G |
|---|---|---|---|---|---|---|---|---|
| | 1 | 2 | 3 | 4 | 5 | 6 | 7 | 8 |
| G Blues Line: | G | | B | | D | E | F♮ | |
| | 1 | | 3 | | 5 | 6 | ♭7 | |

The first part of this example shows this bass line with G as the root (Ex. 10A), then with C as the root (Ex. 10B), with D as the root (Ex. 10C), and finally all three linked together in the typical blues progression (Ex. 10D).

**EXAMPLE 10A – G7 BLUES PATTERN**

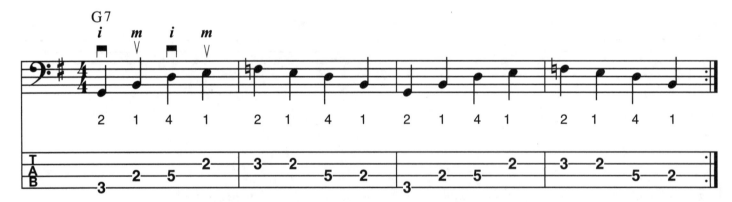

**EXAMPLE 10B – C7 BLUES PATTERN**

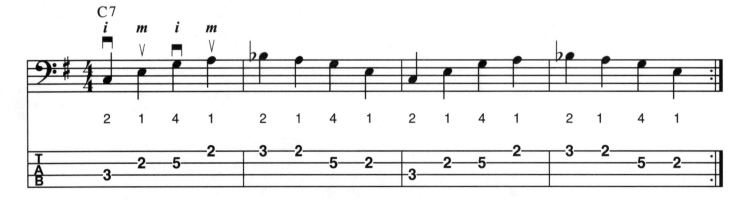

**EXAMPLE 10C – D7 BLUES PATTERN**

Track 28

**EXAMPLE 10D – COMBINATION BLUES PATTERNS – QUARTER NOTES**

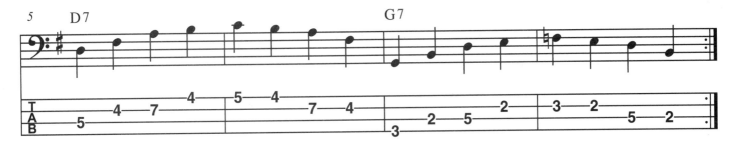

Track 29

**EXAMPLE 11 – COMBINATION BLUES PATTERN – EIGHTH NOTES**

This example is similar to Example 10D, but uses eighth notes instead of quarter notes.
Remember to alternate the right-hand fingering.

Track 30

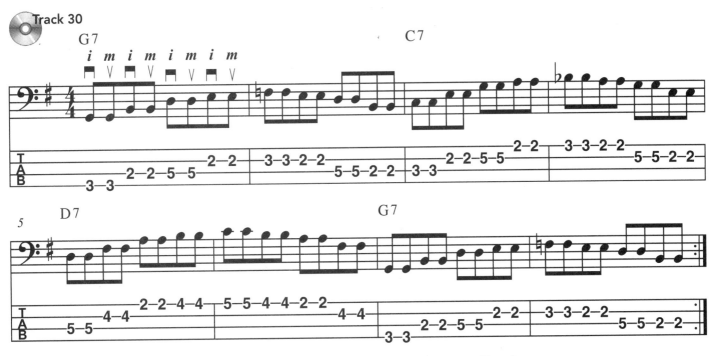

After mastering this bass line, try using it with different notes as the root. Simply start
the pattern on a different note and keep the fingering and fret spacing the same.

### EXAMPLE 12 – COMPLETE BLUES
Track 31

This example uses what is called straight time, where the eighth notes are all even (the same length of time).

Track 32

As you play, listen to the drummer and make sure that your even eighth notes are locked in with his eighth notes. Sometimes the drummer will play eighth notes on the hi-hat, sometimes on the ride cymbal, or fluctuations between the snare and the hi-hat, or the snare and the ride, but just focus on the groove and try to stay even and solid.

**EXAMPLE 13 – SHUFFLE BLUES**

Track 33

The next example uses the same pattern as Example 12, but uses shuffle time instead of straight time. In shuffle time, the eighth notes are no longer evenly spaced, as in straight time, but the first eighth note is a longer length of time than the second eighth note. This only affects the eighth notes, not the quarter notes. Listen to the recorded examples to help better distinguish between straight and shuffle eighth notes.

Track 34

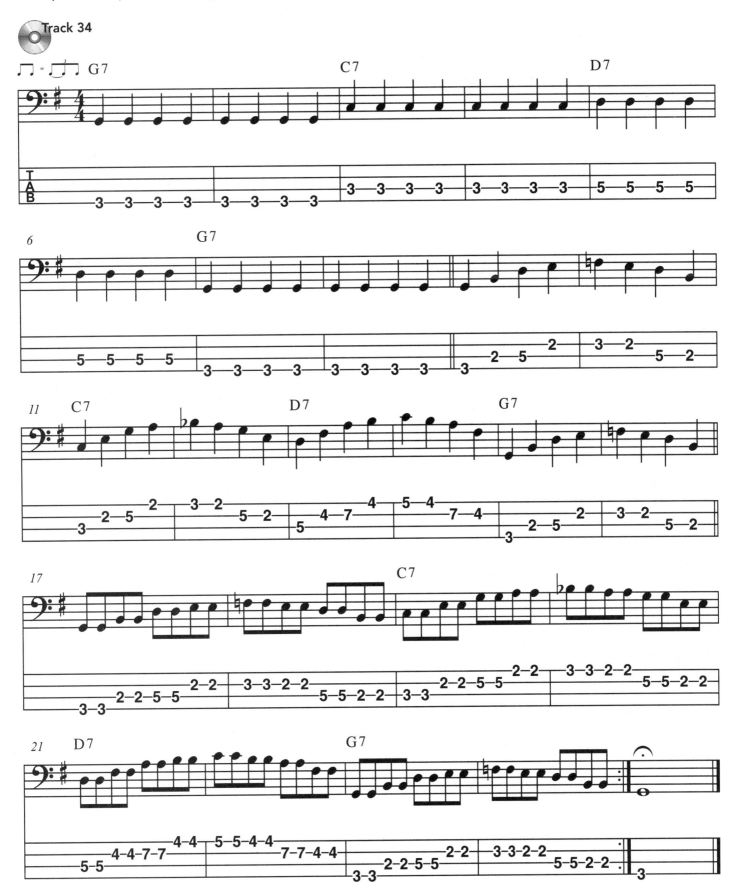

### EXAMPLE 14 – 12-BAR BLUES

Track 35

A common blues progression is the *12-bar blues.* This blues is 12 bars (measures) long and uses the G, C, and D chords. Also, the last two bars contain the **turnaround**. The turnaround comes at the end of a song, and is a chord or series of chords which helps to indicate the end of the form by "turning it around" to the beginning. This turnaround uses a chromatic (all half steps) approach from the third of the G chord (B) to the root of the D chord (D).

Track 36

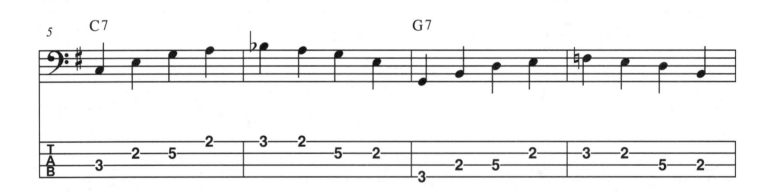

After working on the 12-bar blues in G, try *transposing* it (playing it around the neck in other keys), keeping the same relationship between the notes.

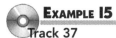

**EXAMPLE 15**
Track 37

Example 15 is a variation on the 12-bar blues and is typical of most rock and roll songs. This example incorporates a similar blues riff to the one used in the 12-bar blues, but varies the pattern a bit. It is also transposed to the key of A, so the open-string notes are used.

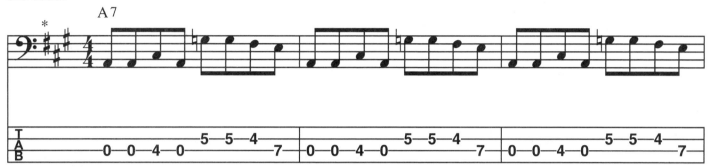

\* Indicates Key of A Major—all Fs, Cs and Gs are sharp.

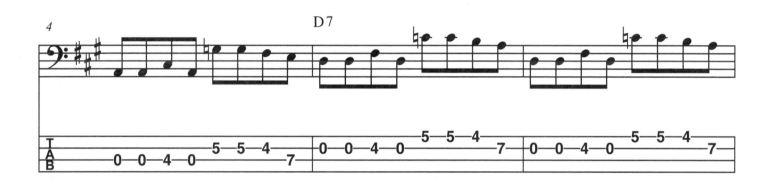

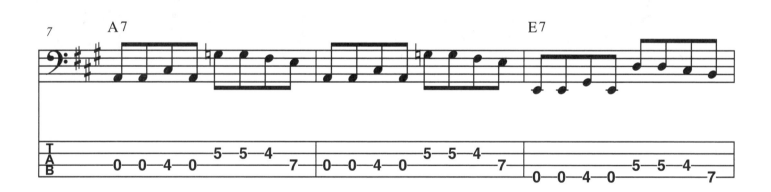

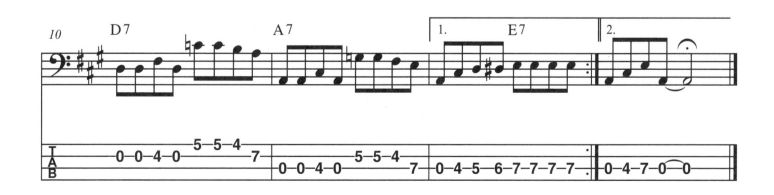

# Slap & Pop Technique

This technique of playing the bass has become very popular in recent years, and mainly requires you to learn to think percussively (like a drummer). The first step is to be able to find the octaves on the bass. An octave is eight notes away from the root, and has the same note name as the root. The octave from any note can be found by moving two strings up and two frets forward. Practice finding all the octaves on the E and A strings by starting with the open strings and working up the neck chromatically.

Track 38

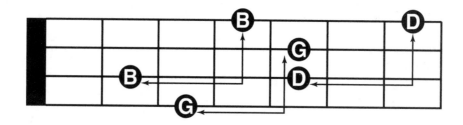

**EXAMPLE 16 – THE SLAP**
Track 39

The next step in this technique is the slap, which is handled by the right-hand thumb. The thumb acts like a hammer, striking the string with the outside of the knuckle, near the area on the bass where the neck meets the body. This can be varied for different sounds; for instance, slapping further back towards the bridge over the pickups gives a brighter, much more open sound, while slapping directly over the neck gives a thinner, tighter sound. The thumb strikes the string, but does not lay on the string. It snaps back away from the string, allowing it to vibrate. Practice slapping the open strings to help establish a good thumb tone.

| T = Thumb |
| --- |

Track 40

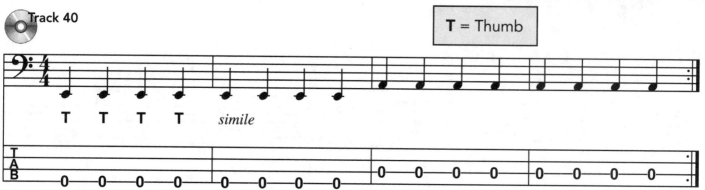

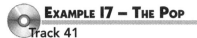

### EXAMPLE 17 – THE POP
Track 41

The final step to learning this technique is the pop, which is done with the right-hand index finger. This is achieved by pulling the string with the tip of the index finger, snapping it away from the fingerboard.

Track 42

**S** = Snap

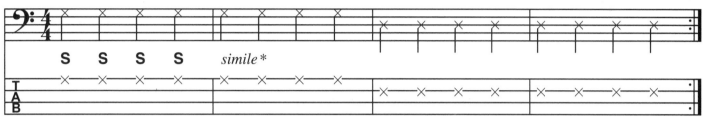

S   S   S   S   *simile**

\* *simile* = Continue the same way.

### EXAMPLE 18
Track 43

This example combines the slap and the pop together. The first part alternates with one slap and one pop. Work on making the slap/pop technique one fluent motion, rather than two separate motions. As the thumb hammers down, the index finger moves into position to snap the string up, moving the hand back into its starting position.

Track 44

### EXAMPLE 18A – COMBINING SLAP AND POP

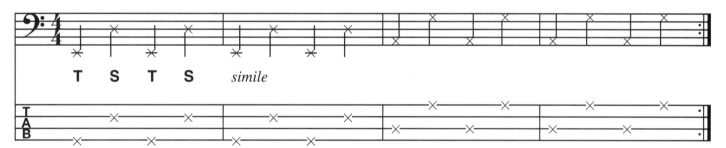

T   S   T   S   *simile*

The next part of this example uses a variation of this technique, combining two slaps together. Since this technique has a very percussive feel to it, try to match what the drummer is playing by matching the slap with the drummer's bass drum and the pop with the drummer's snare. This example uses one slap and one pop, then two slaps and one pop.

Track 45

### EXAMPLE 18B – VARIATION

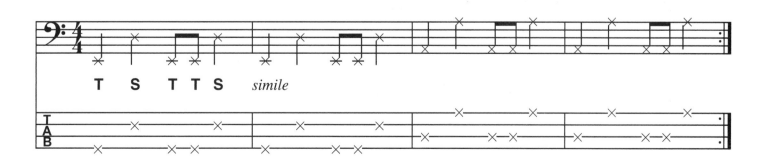

T   S   T   T   S   *simile*

# EXAMPLE 19

Track 46

This example uses the previous technique, but is played over a chord progression, slapping the roots of the chords on the E and A strings and popping the octaves on the D and G strings. The exercise starts with the basic slap/pop technique (Ex. 19A), then incorporates the variation in the right hand (Ex. 19B), and finally a combination of the two (Ex. 19C).

### EXAMPLE 19A – OCTAVE EXERCISE

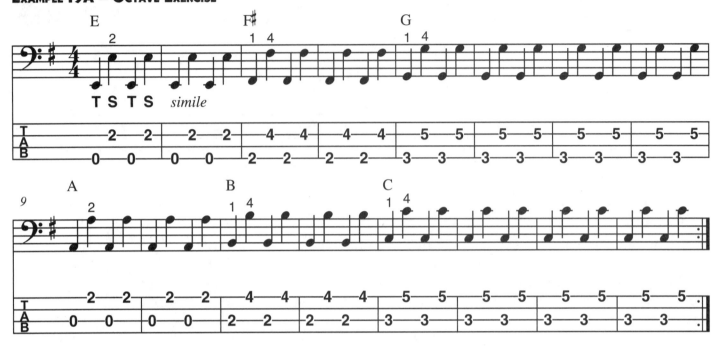

### EXAMPLE 19B – VARIATION

Track 47

EXAMPLE 19C – COMBINATION

T S T S *simile*

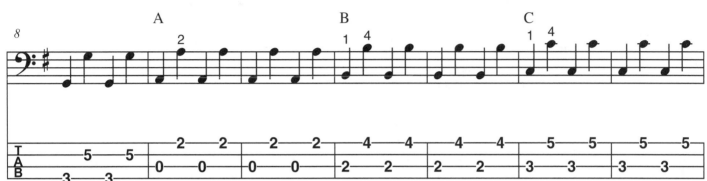

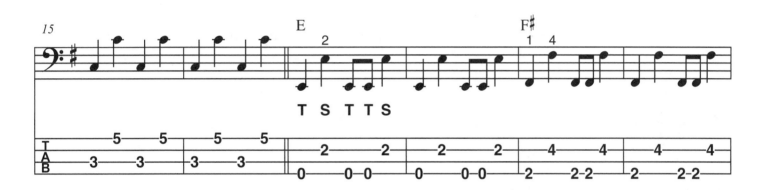

T S T T S

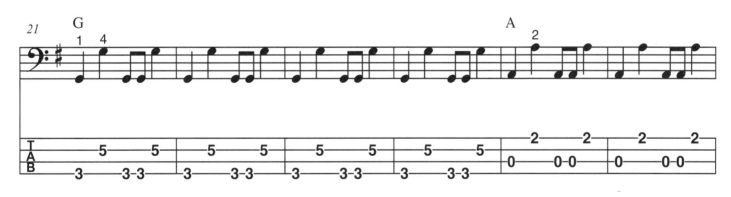

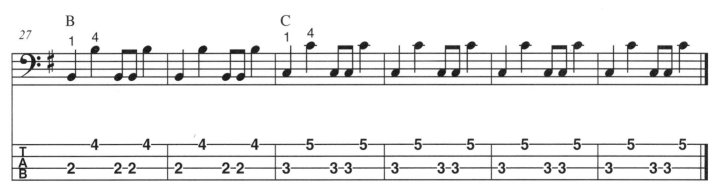

**EXAMPLE 20 – THE HAMMER-ON**
Track 48

This example uses a technique known as the *hammer-on*, where the note is sounded by hammering the string to the fretboard using the tip of any finger of the left hand. The note sounds by the left-hand attack (the right hand is not used). Some strength in the left hand is required to perform this technique; practice it daily so the left- and right-hand attacks sound similar. It is also important to relax; hammering too hard will result in a poor sound.

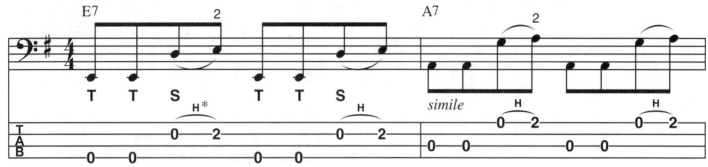

*Hammer note to fretboard w/L.H., indicated by slur (———).

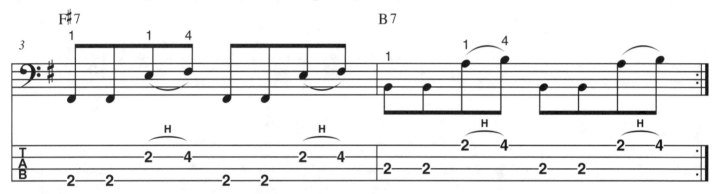

**EXAMPLE 21 – THE PULL-OFF**
Track 49

The *pull-off* is also a left-hand attack technique. Pull the string with the left-hand fingertip as it lifts off the fingerboard (similar to plucking the string with the right hand). Again, practice until the pull-off sounds similar to the right-hand attack.

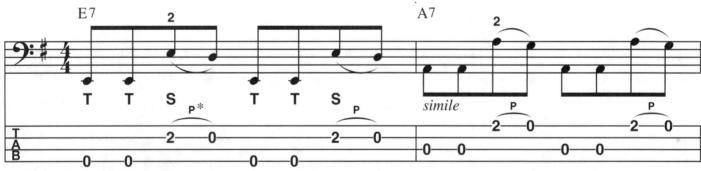

*Pull string w/L.H., indicated by slur (———).

**EXAMPLE 22**

Track 50

This example combines the hammer-on and pull-off techniques. If you're unable to keep up with the recording, practice at a slower tempo with a metronome or drum machine and build the tempo up gradually.

After grasping the information in this book, try moving on to the *Ultimate Beginner Series: Rock Bass Basics* and *Blues Bass Basics* books, covering various styles from rock to blues to country.

# Bass Fingerboard Chart

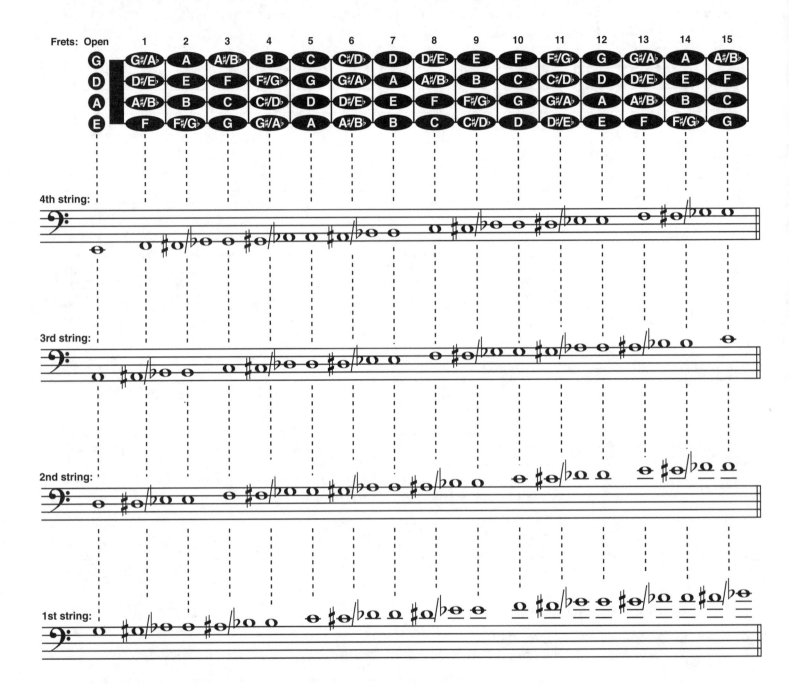